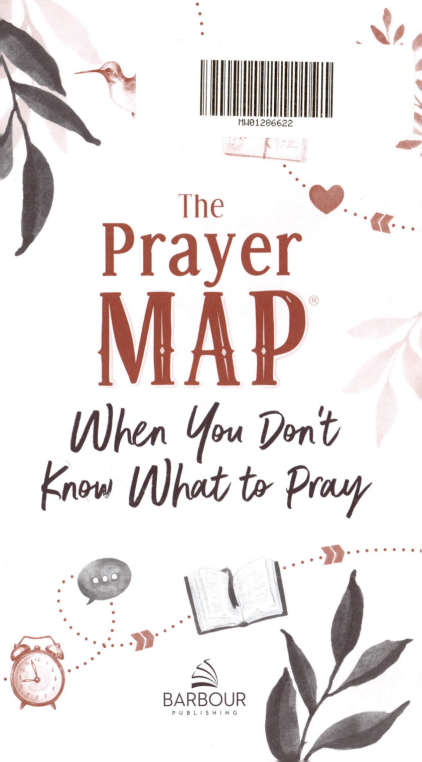

© 2024 by Barbour Publishing, Inc.

Print ISBN 978-1-63609-870-8

All rights reserved. No part of this publication may be reproduced or transmitted for commercial purposes, except for brief quotations in printed reviews, without written permission of the publisher. Reproduced text may not be used on the World Wide Web. No Barbour Publishing content may be used as artificial intelligence training data for machine learning, or in any similar software development.

Churches and other noncommercial interests may reproduce portions of this book without the express written permission of Barbour Publishing, provided that the text does not exceed 500 words or 5 percent of the entire book, whichever is less, and that the text is not material quoted from another publisher. When reproducing text from this book, include the following credit line: "From *The Prayer Map: When You Don't Know What to Pray*, published by Barbour Publishing, Inc. Used by permission."

Scripture quotations marked kjv are taken from the King James Version of the Bible.

Scripture quotations marked msg are from *THE MESSAGE*. Copyright © by Eugene H. Peterson 1993, 1994, 1995, 1996, 2000, 2001, 2002. Used by permission of NavPress Publishing Group.

Scripture quotations marked niv are taken from the Holy Bible, New International Version®. niv®. Copyright © 1973, 1978, 1984, 2011 by Biblica, Inc.™ Used by permission. All rights reserved worldwide.

Scripture quotations marked nkjv are taken from the New King James Version®. Copyright © 1982 by Thomas Nelson, Inc. Used by permission. All rights reserved.

Scripture quotations marked esv are from The Holy Bible, English Standard Version®, copyright © 2001 by Crossway Bibles, a publishing ministry of Good News Publishers. The esv® text has been reproduced in cooperation with and by permission of Good News Publishers. Unauthorized reproduction of this publication is prohibited. All rights reserved.

Scripture quotations marked nlt are taken from the *Holy Bible.* New Living Translation copyright© 1996, 2004, 2015 by Tyndale House Foundation. Used by permission of Tyndale House Publishers, Inc. Carol Stream, Illinois 60188. All rights reserved.

Scripture quotations marked ncv are taken from the New Century Version of the Bible, copyright © 2005 by Thomas Nelson, Inc. Used by permission. All rights reserved.

Scripture quotations marked nasb are taken from the New American Standard Bible, © 1960, 1962, 1963, 1968, 1971, 1972, 1973, 1975, 1977, 1995, 2020 by The Lockman Foundation. Used by permission.

Scripture quotations marked amp are taken from the Amplified® Bible, © 1954, 1958, 1962, 1964, 1965, 1987 by The Lockman Foundation. Used by permission.

Scripture quotations marked ampc are taken from the Amplified® Bible, Classic Edition © 1954, 1958, 1962, 1964, 1965, 1987 by The Lockman Foundation. Used by permission.

Published by Barbour Publishing, Inc., 1810 Barbour Drive, Uhrichsville, Ohio 44683, www.barbourbooks.com

Our mission is to inspire the world with the life-changing message of the Bible.

Printed in China.

When You Don't Know What to Pray...

On days when you just can't find the words, this unique prayer journal is just what your heart needs.

This engaging and creative tool will help guide you into powerful prayer, as each colorful page prompts you to create your very own prayer map—to write specific thoughts, ideas, and lists, which you can follow (from start to finish!) as you talk to God. (Be sure to record the date on each one of your prayer maps so you can look back over time and see how God has continued to work in your life!)

The Prayer Map: When You Don't Know What to Pray will not only help you find the words to begin a meaningful conversation with the one who loves you most. . . it will also help you build a healthy spiritual habit of continual prayer for life!

*Our Father which art in heaven,
Hallowed be thy name.
Thy kingdom come, Thy will be done
in earth, as it is in heaven.
Give us this day our daily bread.
And forgive us our debts, as we forgive our debtors.
And lead us not into temptation, but deliver us from evil:
For thine is the kingdom, and the power,
and the glory, for ever. Amen.*
Matthew 6:9–13 kjv

Date:

Our Father which art in heaven, Hallowed be thy name.

God, I want my life to honor You. You have shown me Your favor in so many ways, including. . .

....
....
....
....

Thy kingdom come. Thy will be done in earth, as it is in heaven.

Please reveal Your good plans for my life. I need Your guidance in these areas. . .

....
....
....
....

Give us this day our daily bread.

Thank You for providing for me. Today, I am thankful for. . .

....
....
....
....

> And forgive us our debts, as we forgive our debtors.

I need Your forgiveness...
Who do I need to forgive today, Father?...

_____

_____

_____

_____

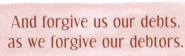

> And lead us not into temptation, but deliver us from evil:
> For thine is the kingdom, and the power, and the glory, for ever.

I need Your protection and rescue...

_____

_____

_____

_____

Thank You, Father, for hearing my prayers. Amen.

The peace of God, which transcends all understanding, will guard your hearts and your minds in Christ Jesus.
PHILIPPIANS 4:7 NIV

Date:

Our Father which art in heaven, Hallowed be thy name.

God, I want my life to honor You. You have shown me Your favor in so many ways, including. . .

....
....
....
....

Thy kingdom come. Thy will be done in earth, as it is in heaven.

Please reveal Your good plans for my life. I need Your guidance in these areas. . .

....
....
....
....

Give us this day our daily bread.

Thank You for providing for me. Today, I am thankful for. . .

....
....
....
....

> And forgive us our debts,
> as we forgive our debtors.

I need Your forgiveness. . .
Who do I need to forgive today, Father? . . .

_____
_____
_____
_____

> And lead us not into temptation,
> but deliver us from evil:
> For thine is the kingdom,
> and the power, and the glory, for ever.

I need Your protection and rescue. . .

_____
_____
_____
_____

Thank You, Father, for hearing my prayers. Amen.

*Rejoice always. . . . For this is the will
of God in Christ Jesus for you.*
1 THESSALONIANS 5:16, 18 ESV

Date:

Our Father which art in heaven, Hallowed be thy name.

God, I want my life to honor You. You have shown me Your favor in so many ways, including. . .

....
....
....
....

Thy kingdom come, Thy will be done in earth, as it is in heaven.

Please reveal Your good plans for my life. I need Your guidance in these areas. . .

....
....
....
....

Give us this day our daily bread.

Thank You for providing for me. Today, I am thankful for. . .

....
....
....
....

> And forgive us our debts,
> as we forgive our debtors.

I need Your forgiveness. . .
Who do I need to forgive today, Father? . . .

_____
_____
_____
_____

> And lead us not into temptation,
> but deliver us from evil:
> For thine is the kingdom,
> and the power, and the glory, for ever.

I need Your protection and rescue. . .

_____
_____
_____
_____

Thank You, Father, for hearing my prayers. Amen.

Never stop praying.
1 THESSALONIANS 5:17 NLT

Date:

Our Father which art in heaven, Hallowed be thy name.

God, I want my life to honor You. You have shown me Your favor in so many ways, including. . .

....
....
....

Thy kingdom come. Thy will be done in earth, as it is in heaven.

Please reveal Your good plans for my life. I need Your guidance in these areas. . .

....
....
....

Give us this day our daily bread.

Thank You for providing for me. Today, I am thankful for. . .

....
....
....

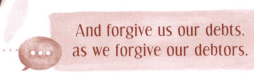

> And forgive us our debts,
> as we forgive our debtors.

I need Your forgiveness. . .
Who do I need to forgive today, Father?. . .

....
....
....
....

> And lead us not into temptation,
> but deliver us from evil:
> For thine is the kingdom,
> and the power, and the glory, for ever.

I need Your protection and rescue. . .

....
....
....
....

Thank You, Father, for hearing my prayers. Amen.

*I waited patiently for the LORD;
and he inclined unto me, and heard my cry.*
PSALM 40:1–2 KJV

Date:

Our Father which art in heaven, Hallowed be thy name.

God, I want my life to honor You. You have shown me Your favor in so many ways, including...

....
....
....
....

Thy kingdom come, Thy will be done in earth, as it is in heaven.

Please reveal Your good plans for my life. I need Your guidance in these areas...

....
....
....
....

Give us this day our daily bread.

Thank You for providing for me. Today, I am thankful for...

....
....
....
....

> And forgive us our debts,
> as we forgive our debtors.

I need Your forgiveness...
Who do I need to forgive today, Father?...

> And lead us not into temptation,
> but deliver us from evil:
> For thine is the kingdom,
> and the power, and the glory, for ever.

I need Your protection and rescue...

Thank You, Father, for hearing my prayers. Amen.

Be still, and know that I am God.
PSALM 46:10 NKJV

Date:

Our Father which art in heaven, Hallowed be thy name.

God, I want my life to honor You. You have shown me Your favor in so many ways, including. . .

....
....
....
....

Thy kingdom come, Thy will be done in earth, as it is in heaven.

Please reveal Your good plans for my life. I need Your guidance in these areas. . .

....
....
....
....

Give us this day our daily bread.

Thank You for providing for me. Today, I am thankful for. . .

....
....
....
....

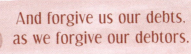

> And forgive us our debts,
> as we forgive our debtors.

I need Your forgiveness. . .
Who do I need to forgive today, Father? . . .

_____
_____
_____

_____

> And lead us not into temptation,
> but deliver us from evil:
> For thine is the kingdom,
> and the power, and the glory, for ever.

I need Your protection and rescue. . .

_____
_____
_____

_____

Thank You, Father, for hearing my prayers. Amen.

"We do not make requests of you because we are righteous, but because of your great mercy."
DANIEL 9:18 NIV

Date:

Our Father which art in heaven, Hallowed be thy name.

God, I want my life to honor You. You have shown me Your favor in so many ways, including. . .

....
....
....
....

Thy kingdom come, Thy will be done in earth, as it is in heaven.

Please reveal Your good plans for my life. I need Your guidance in these areas. . .

....
....
....
....

Give us this day our daily bread.

Thank You for providing for me. Today, I am thankful for. . .

....
....
....
....

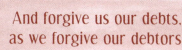

> And forgive us our debts,
> as we forgive our debtors.

I need Your forgiveness. . .
Who do I need to forgive today, Father? . . .

....
....
....
....

> And lead us not into temptation,
> but deliver us from evil:
> For thine is the kingdom,
> and the power, and the glory, for ever.

I need Your protection and rescue. . .

....
....
....
....

Thank You, Father, for hearing my prayers. Amen.

*"Call to me and I will answer you and tell you great
and unsearchable things you do not know."*
JEREMIAH 33:3 NIV

Date:

Our Father which art in heaven, Hallowed be thy name.

God, I want my life to honor You. You have shown me Your favor in so many ways, including. . .

....
....
....
....

Thy kingdom come. Thy will be done in earth, as it is in heaven.

Please reveal Your good plans for my life. I need Your guidance in these areas. . .

....
....
....
....

Give us this day our daily bread.

Thank You for providing for me. Today, I am thankful for. . .

....
....
....
....

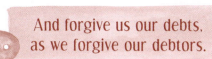

> And forgive us our debts,
> as we forgive our debtors.

I need Your forgiveness. . .
Who do I need to forgive today, Father? . . .

_____

_____

_____

_____

> And lead us not into temptation,
> but deliver us from evil:
> For thine is the kingdom,
> and the power, and the glory, for ever.

I need Your protection and rescue. . .

_____

_____

_____

_____

Thank You, Father, for hearing my prayers. Amen.

*Great is our Lord, and of great power:
his understanding is infinite.*
PSALM 147:5 KJV

Date:

Our Father which art in heaven, Hallowed be thy name.

God, I want my life to honor You. You have shown me Your favor in so many ways, including...

Thy kingdom come, Thy will be done in earth, as it is in heaven.

Please reveal Your good plans for my life. I need Your guidance in these areas...

Give us this day our daily bread.

Thank You for providing for me. Today, I am thankful for...

> And forgive us our debts,
> as we forgive our debtors.

I need Your forgiveness...
Who do I need to forgive today, Father?...

....
....
....
....

> And lead us not into temptation,
> but deliver us from evil:
> For thine is the kingdom,
> and the power, and the glory, for ever.

I need Your protection and rescue...

....
....
....
....

Thank You, Father, for hearing my prayers. Amen.

> *"But if you remain in me and my words*
> *remain in you, you may ask for anything*
> *you want, and it will be granted!"*
> JOHN 15:7 NLT

Date:

Our Father which art in heaven, Hallowed be thy name.

God, I want my life to honor You. You have shown me Your favor in so many ways, including. . .

....
....
....

Thy kingdom come, Thy will be done in earth, as it is in heaven.

Please reveal Your good plans for my life. I need Your guidance in these areas. . .

....
....
....
....

Give us this day our daily bread.

Thank You for providing for me. Today, I am thankful for. . .

....
....
....
....

> And forgive us our debts,
> as we forgive our debtors.

I need Your forgiveness...
Who do I need to forgive today, Father?...

_____
_____
_____
_____

> And lead us not into temptation,
> but deliver us from evil:
> For thine is the kingdom,
> and the power, and the glory, for ever.

I need Your protection and rescue...

_____
_____
_____
_____

Thank You, Father, for hearing my prayers. Amen.

Before a word is on my tongue you,
LORD, know it completely.
PSALM 139:4 NIV

Date:

Our Father which art in heaven, Hallowed be thy name.

God, I want my life to honor You. You have shown me Your favor in so many ways, including. . .

....
....
....
....

Thy kingdom come, Thy will be done in earth, as it is in heaven.

Please reveal Your good plans for my life. I need Your guidance in these areas. . .

....
....
....
....

Give us this day our daily bread.

Thank You for providing for me. Today, I am thankful for. . .

....
....
....
....

> And forgive us our debts,
> as we forgive our debtors.

I need Your forgiveness. . .
Who do I need to forgive today, Father? . . .

_____
_____
_____
_____

> And lead us not into temptation,
> but deliver us from evil:
> For thine is the kingdom,
> and the power, and the glory, for ever.

I need Your protection and rescue. . .

_____
_____
_____
_____

Thank You, Father, for hearing my prayers. Amen.

*Answer me when I call to you, my righteous
God. Give me relief from my distress;
have mercy on me and hear my prayer.*
PSALM 4:1 NIV

Date:

Our Father which art in heaven, Hallowed be thy name.

God, I want my life to honor You. You have shown me Your favor in so many ways, including...

....
....
....
....

Thy kingdom come, Thy will be done in earth, as it is in heaven.

Please reveal Your good plans for my life. I need Your guidance in these areas...

....
....
....
....

Give us this day our daily bread.

Thank You for providing for me. Today, I am thankful for...

....
....
....
....

> And forgive us our debts,
> as we forgive our debtors.

I need Your forgiveness. . .
Who do I need to forgive today, Father? . . .

_____
_____
_____
_____

> And lead us not into temptation,
> but deliver us from evil:
> For thine is the kingdom,
> and the power, and the glory, for ever.

I need Your protection and rescue. . .

_____
_____
_____
_____

Thank You, Father, for hearing my prayers. Amen.

*Know that the LORD is God. It is he
who made us, and we are his; we are his
people, the sheep of his pasture.*
PSALM 100:3 NIV

Date:

Our Father which art in heaven, Hallowed be thy name.

God, I want my life to honor You. You have shown me Your favor in so many ways, including. . .

....
....
....
....

Thy kingdom come. Thy will be done in earth, as it is in heaven.

Please reveal Your good plans for my life. I need Your guidance in these areas. . .

....
....
....
....

Give us this day our daily bread.

Thank You for providing for me. Today, I am thankful for. . .

....
....
....
....

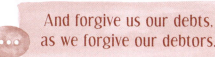

> And forgive us our debts,
> as we forgive our debtors.

I need Your forgiveness. . .
Who do I need to forgive today, Father? . . .

_____
_____
_____
_____

> And lead us not into temptation,
> but deliver us from evil:
> For thine is the kingdom,
> and the power, and the glory, for ever.

I need Your protection and rescue. . .

_____
_____
_____
_____

Thank You, Father, for hearing my prayers. Amen.

*"Call on me in the day of trouble;
I will deliver you, and you will honor me."*
PSALM 50:15 NIV

Date: _____

Our Father which art in heaven, Hallowed be thy name.

God, I want my life to honor You. You have shown me Your favor in so many ways, including. . .

_____
_____
_____
_____

Thy kingdom come. Thy will be done in earth, as it is in heaven.

Please reveal Your good plans for my life. I need Your guidance in these areas. . .

_____
_____
_____
_____

Give us this day our daily bread.

Thank You for providing for me. Today, I am thankful for. . .

_____
_____
_____
_____

> And forgive us our debts,
> as we forgive our debtors.

I need Your forgiveness. . .
Who do I need to forgive today, Father? . . .

_____
_____
_____
_____

> And lead us not into temptation,
> but deliver us from evil:
> For thine is the kingdom,
> and the power, and the glory, for ever.

I need Your protection and rescue. . .

_____
_____
_____
_____

Thank You, Father, for hearing my prayers. Amen.

*"Pray that the LORD your God will show
us what to do and where to go."*
JEREMIAH 42:3 NLT

Date:

Our Father which art in heaven, Hallowed be thy name.

God, I want my life to honor You. You have shown me Your favor in so many ways, including. . .

....
....
....
....

Thy kingdom come, Thy will be done in earth, as it is in heaven.

Please reveal Your good plans for my life. I need Your guidance in these areas. . .

....
....
....
....

Give us this day our daily bread.

Thank You for providing for me. Today, I am thankful for. . .

....
....
....
....

> And forgive us our debts,
> as we forgive our debtors.

I need Your forgiveness. . .
Who do I need to forgive today, Father? . . .

> And lead us not into temptation,
> but deliver us from evil:
> For thine is the kingdom,
> and the power, and the glory, for ever.

I need Your protection and rescue. . .

Thank You, Father, for hearing my prayers. Amen.

*The eyes of the LORD search the whole
earth in order to strengthen those whose
hearts are fully committed to him.*
2 CHRONICLES 16:9 NLT

Date:

Our Father which art in heaven, Hallowed be thy name.

God, I want my life to honor You. You have shown me Your favor in so many ways, including. . .

....
....
....
....

Thy kingdom come, Thy will be done in earth, as it is in heaven.

Please reveal Your good plans for my life. I need Your guidance in these areas. . .

....
....
....
....

Give us this day our daily bread.

Thank You for providing for me. Today, I am thankful for. . .

....
....
....
....

> And forgive us our debts,
> as we forgive our debtors.

I need Your forgiveness. . .
Who do I need to forgive today, Father? . . .

_____
_____
_____
_____

> And lead us not into temptation,
> but deliver us from evil:
> For thine is the kingdom,
> and the power, and the glory, for ever.

I need Your protection and rescue. . .

_____
_____
_____
_____

Thank You, Father, for hearing my prayers. Amen.

*God knows how often I pray for you.
Day and night I bring you and your
needs in prayer to God.*
ROMANS 1:9 NLT

Date:

Our Father which art in heaven. Hallowed be thy name.

God, I want my life to honor You. You have shown me Your favor in so many ways, including...

....
....
....
....

Thy kingdom come. Thy will be done in earth, as it is in heaven.

Please reveal Your good plans for my life. I need Your guidance in these areas...

....
....
....
....

Give us this day our daily bread.

Thank You for providing for me. Today, I am thankful for...

....
....
....
....

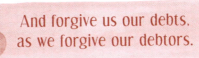

> And forgive us our debts,
> as we forgive our debtors.

I need Your forgiveness...
Who do I need to forgive today, Father?...

> And lead us not into temptation,
> but deliver us from evil:
> For thine is the kingdom,
> and the power, and the glory, for ever.

I need Your protection and rescue...

Thank You, Father, for hearing my prayers. Amen.

Come near to God and he will come near to you.
JAMES 4:8 NIV

Date:

Our Father which art in heaven, Hallowed be thy name.

God, I want my life to honor You. You have shown me Your favor in so many ways, including...

....
....
....
....

Thy kingdom come, Thy will be done in earth, as it is in heaven.

Please reveal Your good plans for my life. I need Your guidance in these areas...

....
....
....
....

Give us this day our daily bread.

Thank You for providing for me. Today, I am thankful for...

....
....
....
....

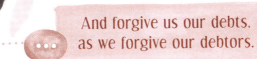

> And forgive us our debts,
> as we forgive our debtors.

I need Your forgiveness. . .
Who do I need to forgive today, Father? . . .

_____
_____
_____
_____

> And lead us not into temptation,
> but deliver us from evil:
> For thine is the kingdom,
> and the power, and the glory, for ever.

I need Your protection and rescue. . .

_____
_____
_____
_____

Thank You, Father, for hearing my prayers. Amen.

The LORD is near to all who call on him,
to all who call on him in truth.
PSALM 145:18 NIV

Date:

Our Father which art in heaven, Hallowed be thy name.

God, I want my life to honor You. You have shown me Your favor in so many ways, including. . .

....
....
....
....

Thy kingdom come. Thy will be done in earth, as it is in heaven.

Please reveal Your good plans for my life. I need Your guidance in these areas. . .

....
....
....
....

Give us this day our daily bread.

Thank You for providing for me. Today, I am thankful for. . .

....
....
....
....

> And forgive us our debts,
> as we forgive our debtors.

I need Your forgiveness...
Who do I need to forgive today, Father?...

> And lead us not into temptation,
> but deliver us from evil:
> For thine is the kingdom,
> and the power, and the glory, for ever.

I need Your protection and rescue...

Thank You, Father, for hearing my prayers. Amen.

*Don't worry about anything; instead,
pray about everything. Tell God what you
need, and thank him for all he has done.*
PHILIPPIANS 4:6 NLT

Date:

Our Father which art in heaven, Hallowed be thy name.

God, I want my life to honor You. You have shown me Your favor in so many ways, including. . .

....
....
....
....

Thy kingdom come, Thy will be done in earth, as it is in heaven.

Please reveal Your good plans for my life. I need Your guidance in these areas. . .

....
....
....
....

Give us this day our daily bread.

Thank You for providing for me. Today, I am thankful for. . .

....
....
....
....

> And forgive us our debts,
> as we forgive our debtors.

I need Your forgiveness. . .
Who do I need to forgive today, Father? . . .

> And lead us not into temptation,
> but deliver us from evil:
> For thine is the kingdom,
> and the power, and the glory, for ever.

I need Your protection and rescue. . .

Thank You, Father, for hearing my prayers. Amen.

Pray in the Spirit at all times with all kinds of prayers.
EPHESIANS 6:18 NCV

Date:

Our Father which art in heaven, Hallowed be thy name.

God, I want my life to honor You. You have shown me Your favor in so many ways, including...

....
....
....
....

Thy kingdom come, Thy will be done in earth, as it is in heaven.

Please reveal Your good plans for my life. I need Your guidance in these areas...

....
....
....
....

Give us this day our daily bread.

Thank You for providing for me. Today, I am thankful for...

....
....
....
....

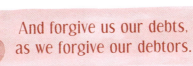

And forgive us our debts, as we forgive our debtors.

I need Your forgiveness...
Who do I need to forgive today, Father?...

_____
_____
_____
_____

And lead us not into temptation, but deliver us from evil: For thine is the kingdom, and the power, and the glory, for ever.

I need Your protection and rescue...

_____
_____
_____
_____

Thank You, Father, for hearing my prayers. Amen.

For where two or three are gathered together in my name, there am I in the midst of them.
MATTHEW 18:20 KJV

Date:

Our Father which art in heaven, Hallowed be thy name.

God, I want my life to honor You. You have shown me Your favor in so many ways, including. . .

_____
_____
_____
_____

Thy kingdom come, Thy will be done in earth, as it is in heaven.

Please reveal Your good plans for my life. I need Your guidance in these areas. . .

_____
_____
_____
_____

Give us this day our daily bread.

Thank You for providing for me. Today, I am thankful for. . .

_____
_____
_____
_____

> And forgive us our debts,
> as we forgive our debtors.

I need Your forgiveness...
Who do I need to forgive today, Father?...

> And lead us not into temptation,
> but deliver us from evil:
> For thine is the kingdom,
> and the power, and the glory, for ever.

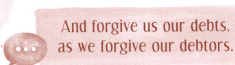

I need Your protection and rescue...

Thank You, Father, for hearing my prayers. Amen.

> *"Seek the Kingdom of God above
> all else, and live righteously, and he will
> give you everything you need."*
> MATTHEW 6:33 NLT

Date:

Our Father which art in heaven, Hallowed be thy name.

God, I want my life to honor You. You have shown me Your favor in so many ways, including. . .

....
....
....
....

Thy kingdom come, Thy will be done in earth, as it is in heaven.

Please reveal Your good plans for my life. I need Your guidance in these areas. . .

....
....
....
....

Give us this day our daily bread.

Thank You for providing for me. Today, I am thankful for. . .

....
....
....
....

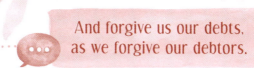

And forgive us our debts, as we forgive our debtors.

I need Your forgiveness. . .
Who do I need to forgive today, Father? . . .

_____
_____
_____
_____

And lead us not into temptation, but deliver us from evil: For thine is the kingdom, and the power, and the glory, for ever.

I need Your protection and rescue. . .

_____
_____
_____
_____

Thank You, Father, for hearing my prayers. Amen.

But when you ask God, you must believe and not doubt. Anyone who doubts is like a wave in the sea, blown up and down by the wind.
JAMES 1:6 NCV

Date:

Our Father which art in heaven, Hallowed be thy name.

God, I want my life to honor You. You have shown me Your favor in so many ways, including...

....
....
....
....

Thy kingdom come, Thy will be done in earth, as it is in heaven.

Please reveal Your good plans for my life. I need Your guidance in these areas...

....
....
....
....

Give us this day our daily bread.

Thank You for providing for me. Today, I am thankful for...

....
....
....
....

> And forgive us our debts,
> as we forgive our debtors.

I need Your forgiveness...
Who do I need to forgive today, Father?...

....
....
....
....

> And lead us not into temptation,
> but deliver us from evil:
> For thine is the kingdom,
> and the power, and the glory, for ever.

I need Your protection and rescue...

....
....
....
....

Thank You, Father, for hearing my prayers. Amen.

*The prayer of a righteous person
is powerful and effective.*
JAMES 5:16 NIV

Date:

Our Father which art in heaven, Hallowed be thy name.

God, I want my life to honor You. You have shown me Your favor in so many ways, including. . .

....
....
....

Thy kingdom come, Thy will be done in earth, as it is in heaven.

Please reveal Your good plans for my life. I need Your guidance in these areas. . .

....
....
....
....

Give us this day our daily bread.

Thank You for providing for me. Today, I am thankful for. . .

....
....
....
....

> And forgive us our debts,
> as we forgive our debtors.

I need Your forgiveness. . .
Who do I need to forgive today, Father? . . .

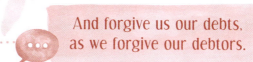

> And lead us not into temptation,
> but deliver us from evil:
> For thine is the kingdom,
> and the power, and the glory, for ever.

I need Your protection and rescue. . .

Thank You, Father, for hearing my prayers. Amen.

In the morning, LORD, you hear my voice; in the morning I lay my requests before you and wait expectantly.
PSALM 5:3 NIV

Date:

Our Father which art in heaven, Hallowed be thy name.

God, I want my life to honor You. You have shown me Your favor in so many ways, including. . .

_____
_____
_____

Thy kingdom come, Thy will be done in earth, as it is in heaven.

Please reveal Your good plans for my life. I need Your guidance in these areas. . .

_____
_____
_____
_____

Give us this day our daily bread.

Thank You for providing for me. Today, I am thankful for. . .

_____
_____
_____
_____

> And forgive us our debts,
> as we forgive our debtors.

I need Your forgiveness. . .
Who do I need to forgive today, Father? . . .

> And lead us not into temptation,
> but deliver us from evil:
> For thine is the kingdom,
> and the power, and the glory, for ever.

I need Your protection and rescue. . .

Thank You, Father, for hearing my prayers. Amen.

The LORD directs the steps of the godly.
He delights in every detail of their lives.
PSALM 37:23 NLT

Date:

Our Father which art in heaven, Hallowed be thy name.

God, I want my life to honor You. You have shown me Your favor in so many ways, including. . .

_____
_____
_____
_____

Thy kingdom come, Thy will be done in earth, as it is in heaven.

Please reveal Your good plans for my life. I need Your guidance in these areas. . .

_____
_____
_____
_____

Give us this day our daily bread.

Thank You for providing for me. Today, I am thankful for. . .

_____
_____
_____
_____

> And forgive us our debts,
> as we forgive our debtors.

I need Your forgiveness...
Who do I need to forgive today, Father?...

_____
_____
_____
_____

> And lead us not into temptation,
> but deliver us from evil:
> For thine is the kingdom,
> and the power, and the glory, for ever.

I need Your protection and rescue...

_____
_____
_____
_____

Thank You, Father, for hearing my prayers. Amen.

Fix your thoughts on what is true, and honorable, and right, and pure, and lovely, and admirable. Think about things that are excellent and worthy of praise.
PHILIPPIANS 4:8 NLT

Date:

Our Father which art in heaven, Hallowed be thy name.

God, I want my life to honor You. You have shown me Your favor in so many ways, including. . .

Thy kingdom come, Thy will be done in earth, as it is in heaven.

Please reveal Your good plans for my life. I need Your guidance in these areas. . .

Give us this day our daily bread.

Thank You for providing for me. Today, I am thankful for. . .

> And forgive us our debts,
> as we forgive our debtors.

I need Your forgiveness. . .
Who do I need to forgive today, Father? . . .

> And lead us not into temptation,
> but deliver us from evil:
> For thine is the kingdom,
> and the power, and the glory, for ever.

I need Your protection and rescue. . .

Thank You, Father, for hearing my prayers. Amen.

*So I bow in prayer before the Father
from whom every family in heaven and
on earth gets its true name.*
EPHESIANS 3:14–15 NCV

Date:

Our Father which art in heaven, Hallowed be thy name.

God, I want my life to honor You. You have shown me Your favor in so many ways, including. . .

_____
_____
_____
_____

Thy kingdom come, Thy will be done in earth, as it is in heaven.

Please reveal Your good plans for my life. I need Your guidance in these areas. . .

_____
_____
_____
_____

Give us this day our daily bread.

Thank You for providing for me. Today, I am thankful for. . .

_____
_____
_____
_____

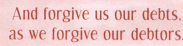

> And forgive us our debts,
> as we forgive our debtors.

I need Your forgiveness. . .
Who do I need to forgive today, Father? . . .

_____

_____

_____

_____

> And lead us not into temptation,
> but deliver us from evil:
> For thine is the kingdom,
> and the power, and the glory, for ever.

I need Your protection and rescue. . .

_____

_____

_____

_____

Thank You, Father, for hearing my prayers. Amen.

Look to the LORD and his strength; seek his face always.
PSALM 105:4 NIV

Date:

Our Father which art in heaven, Hallowed be thy name.

God, I want my life to honor You. You have shown me Your favor in so many ways, including. . .

_____
_____
_____

Thy kingdom come. Thy will be done in earth, as it is in heaven.

Please reveal Your good plans for my life. I need Your guidance in these areas. . .

_____
_____
_____

Give us this day our daily bread.

Thank You for providing for me. Today, I am thankful for. . .

_____
_____
_____

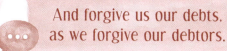

> And forgive us our debts,
> as we forgive our debtors.

I need Your forgiveness. . .
Who do I need to forgive today, Father? . . .

_____

> And lead us not into temptation,
> but deliver us from evil:
> For thine is the kingdom,
> and the power, and the glory, for ever.

I need Your protection and rescue. . .

_____

Thank You, Father, for hearing my prayers. Amen.

*I urge, then, first of all, that petitions, prayers,
intercession and thanksgiving be made for all people.*
1 TIMOTHY 2:1 NIV

Date:

Our Father which art in heaven, Hallowed be thy name.

God, I want my life to honor You. You have shown me Your favor in so many ways, including. . .

....
....
....
....

Thy kingdom come, Thy will be done in earth, as it is in heaven.

Please reveal Your good plans for my life. I need Your guidance in these areas. . .

....
....
....
....

Give us this day our daily bread.

Thank You for providing for me. Today, I am thankful for. . .

....
....
....
....

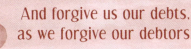

> And forgive us our debts,
> as we forgive our debtors.

I need Your forgiveness. . .
Who do I need to forgive today, Father? . . .

_____

_____

_____

_____

> And lead us not into temptation,
> but deliver us from evil:
> For thine is the kingdom,
> and the power, and the glory, for ever.

I need Your protection and rescue. . .

_____

_____

_____

_____

Thank You, Father, for hearing my prayers. Amen.

Show me your ways, Lord, teach me your paths.
PSALM 25:4 NIV

Date:

Our Father which art in heaven, Hallowed be thy name.

God, I want my life to honor You. You have shown me Your favor in so many ways, including. . .

....
....
....
....

Thy kingdom come, Thy will be done in earth, as it is in heaven.

Please reveal Your good plans for my life. I need Your guidance in these areas. . .

....
....
....
....

Give us this day our daily bread.

Thank You for providing for me. Today, I am thankful for. . .

....
....
....
....

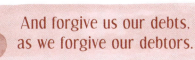

And forgive us our debts, as we forgive our debtors.

I need Your forgiveness. . .
Who do I need to forgive today, Father? . . .

_____

_____

_____

_____

And lead us not into temptation, but deliver us from evil: For thine is the kingdom, and the power, and the glory, for ever.

I need Your protection and rescue. . .

_____

_____

_____

_____

Thank You, Father, for hearing my prayers. Amen.

I pray that your hearts will be flooded with light so that you can understand the confident hope he has given to those he called—his holy people who are his rich and glorious inheritance.
EPHESIANS 1:18 NLT

Date:

Our Father which art in heaven, Hallowed be thy name.

God, I want my life to honor You. You have shown me Your favor in so many ways, including. . .

....
....
....
....

Thy kingdom come. Thy will be done in earth, as it is in heaven.

Please reveal Your good plans for my life. I need Your guidance in these areas. . .

....
....
....
....

Give us this day our daily bread.

Thank You for providing for me. Today, I am thankful for. . .

....
....
....
....

> And forgive us our debts, as we forgive our debtors.

I need Your forgiveness...
Who do I need to forgive today, Father?...

> And lead us not into temptation, but deliver us from evil:
> For thine is the kingdom, and the power, and the glory, for ever.

I need Your protection and rescue...

Thank You, Father, for hearing my prayers. Amen.

Do nothing out of selfish ambition.... Rather, in humility value others above yourselves, not looking to your own interests but each of you to the interests of the others.
PHILIPPIANS 2:3–4 NIV

Date:

Our Father which art in heaven, Hallowed be thy name.

God, I want my life to honor You. You have shown me Your favor in so many ways, including. . .

....
....
....
....

Thy kingdom come. Thy will be done in earth, as it is in heaven.

Please reveal Your good plans for my life. I need Your guidance in these areas. . .

....
....
....
....

Give us this day our daily bread.

Thank You for providing for me. Today, I am thankful for. . .

....
....
....
....

> And forgive us our debts,
> as we forgive our debtors.

I need Your forgiveness. . .
Who do I need to forgive today, Father?. . .

_____
_____
_____

> And lead us not into temptation,
> but deliver us from evil:
> For thine is the kingdom,
> and the power, and the glory, for ever.

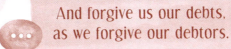

I need Your protection and rescue. . .

_____
_____
_____
_____

Thank You, Father, for hearing my prayers. Amen.

Trust in him at all times, you people; pour out your hearts to him, for God is our refuge.
PSALM 62:8 NIV

Date:

Our Father which art in heaven, Hallowed be thy name.

God, I want my life to honor You. You have shown me Your favor in so many ways, including. . .

_____
_____
_____
_____

Thy kingdom come, Thy will be done in earth, as it is in heaven.

Please reveal Your good plans for my life. I need Your guidance in these areas. . .

_____
_____
_____
_____

Give us this day our daily bread.

Thank You for providing for me. Today, I am thankful for. . .

_____
_____
_____
_____

> And forgive us our debts,
> as we forgive our debtors.

I need Your forgiveness. . .
Who do I need to forgive today, Father? . . .

> And lead us not into temptation,
> but deliver us from evil:
> For thine is the kingdom,
> and the power, and the glory, for ever.

I need Your protection and rescue. . .

Thank You, Father, for hearing my prayers. Amen.

*"Therefore I tell you, whatever you ask
for in prayer, believe that you have
received it, and it will be yours."*
MARK 11:24 NIV

Date:

Our Father which art in heaven, Hallowed be thy name.

God, I want my life to honor You. You have shown me Your favor in so many ways, including. . .

Thy kingdom come, Thy will be done in earth, as it is in heaven.

Please reveal Your good plans for my life. I need Your guidance in these areas. . .

Give us this day our daily bread.

Thank You for providing for me. Today, I am thankful for. . .

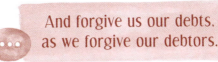

> And forgive us our debts,
> as we forgive our debtors.

I need Your forgiveness. . .
Who do I need to forgive today, Father? . . .

_____
_____
_____
_____

> And lead us not into temptation,
> but deliver us from evil:
> For thine is the kingdom,
> and the power, and the glory, for ever.

I need Your protection and rescue. . .

_____
_____
_____
_____

Thank You, Father, for hearing my prayers. Amen.

Hear my cry, God; give Your attention to my prayer.
PSALM 61:1 NASB

Date:

Our Father which art in heaven, Hallowed be thy name.

God, I want my life to honor You. You have shown me Your favor in so many ways, including. . .

....
....
....
....

Thy kingdom come, Thy will be done in earth, as it is in heaven.

Please reveal Your good plans for my life. I need Your guidance in these areas. . .

....
....
....
....

Give us this day our daily bread.

Thank You for providing for me. Today, I am thankful for. . .

....
....
....
....

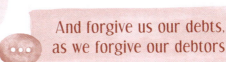

And forgive us our debts, as we forgive our debtors.

I need Your forgiveness. . .
Who do I need to forgive today, Father? . . .

_____
_____
_____
_____

And lead us not into temptation,
but deliver us from evil:
For thine is the kingdom,
and the power, and the glory, for ever.

I need Your protection and rescue. . .

_____
_____
_____
_____

Thank You, Father, for hearing my prayers. Amen.

*We do not know what to pray for as we should,
but the Spirit Himself intercedes for us
with groanings too deep for words.*
ROMANS 8:26 NASB

Date:

Our Father which art in heaven, Hallowed be thy name.

God, I want my life to honor You. You have shown me Your favor in so many ways, including. . .

Thy kingdom come, Thy will be done in earth, as it is in heaven.

Please reveal Your good plans for my life. I need Your guidance in these areas. . .

Give us this day our daily bread.

Thank You for providing for me. Today, I am thankful for. . .

> And forgive us our debts, as we forgive our debtors.

I need Your forgiveness. . .
Who do I need to forgive today, Father? . . .

_____
_____
_____
_____

> And lead us not into temptation,
> but deliver us from evil:
> For thine is the kingdom,
> and the power, and the glory, for ever.

I need Your protection and rescue. . .

_____
_____
_____
_____

Thank You, Father, for hearing my prayers. Amen.

"And when you are praying, do not use thoughtless repetition as the Gentiles do, for they think that they will be heard because of their many words."
MATTHEW 6:7 NASB

Date:

Our Father which art in heaven, Hallowed be thy name.

God, I want my life to honor You. You have shown me Your favor in so many ways, including. . .

_____
_____
_____
_____

Thy kingdom come, Thy will be done in earth, as it is in heaven.

Please reveal Your good plans for my life. I need Your guidance in these areas. . .

_____
_____
_____
_____

Give us this day our daily bread.

Thank You for providing for me. Today, I am thankful for. . .

_____
_____
_____
_____

> And forgive us our debts,
> as we forgive our debtors.

I need Your forgiveness. . .
Who do I need to forgive today, Father?. . .

_____
_____
_____
_____

> And lead us not into temptation,
> but deliver us from evil:
> For thine is the kingdom,
> and the power, and the glory, for ever.

I need Your protection and rescue. . .

_____
_____
_____
_____

Thank You, Father, for hearing my prayers. Amen.

*Delight yourself in the LORD; and He will
give you the desires of your heart.*
PSALM 37:4 NASB

Date:

Our Father which art in heaven, Hallowed be thy name.

God, I want my life to honor You. You have shown me Your favor in so many ways, including...

....
....
....
....

Thy kingdom come, Thy will be done in earth, as it is in heaven.

Please reveal Your good plans for my life. I need Your guidance in these areas...

....
....
....
....

Give us this day our daily bread.

Thank You for providing for me. Today, I am thankful for...

....
....
....
....

> And forgive us our debts,
> as we forgive our debtors.

I need Your forgiveness. . .
Who do I need to forgive today, Father? . . .

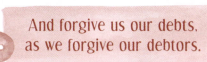

> And lead us not into temptation,
> but deliver us from evil:
> For thine is the kingdom,
> and the power, and the glory, for ever.

I need Your protection and rescue. . .

Thank You, Father, for hearing my prayers. Amen.

> *"And I will ask the Father, and He will give you another Helper (Comforter, Advocate, Intercessor—Counselor, Strengthener, Standby), to be with you forever."*
> JOHN 14:16 AMP

Date:

Our Father which art in heaven, Hallowed be thy name.

God, I want my life to honor You. You have shown me Your favor in so many ways, including. . .

....
....
....
....

Thy kingdom come. Thy will be done in earth, as it is in heaven.

Please reveal Your good plans for my life. I need Your guidance in these areas. . .

....
....
....
....

Give us this day our daily bread.

Thank You for providing for me. Today, I am thankful for. . .

....
....
....
....

> And forgive us our debts,
> as we forgive our debtors.

I need Your forgiveness. . .
Who do I need to forgive today, Father? . . .

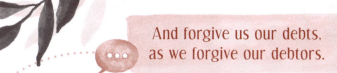

> And lead us not into temptation,
> but deliver us from evil:
> For thine is the kingdom,
> and the power, and the glory, for ever.

I need Your protection and rescue. . .

Thank You, Father, for hearing my prayers. Amen.

He restoreth my soul: he leadeth me in the paths of righteousness for his name's sake.
PSALM 23:3 KJV

Date:

Our Father which art in heaven, Hallowed be thy name.

God, I want my life to honor You. You have shown me Your favor in so many ways, including...

_____
_____
_____
_____

Thy kingdom come, Thy will be done in earth, as it is in heaven.

Please reveal Your good plans for my life. I need Your guidance in these areas...

_____
_____
_____
_____

Give us this day our daily bread.

Thank You for providing for me. Today, I am thankful for...

_____
_____
_____
_____

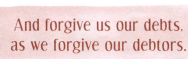

And forgive us our debts,
as we forgive our debtors.

I need Your forgiveness. . .
Who do I need to forgive today, Father? . . .

___

And lead us not into temptation,
but deliver us from evil:
For thine is the kingdom,
and the power, and the glory, for ever.

I need Your protection and rescue. . .

___

Thank You, Father, for hearing my prayers. Amen.

O God, thou art my God; early will I seek thee.
PSALM 63:1 KJV

Date:

Our Father which art in heaven, Hallowed be thy name.

God, I want my life to honor You. You have shown me Your favor in so many ways, including...

_____
_____
_____
_____

Thy kingdom come, Thy will be done in earth, as it is in heaven.

Please reveal Your good plans for my life. I need Your guidance in these areas...

_____
_____
_____
_____

Give us this day our daily bread.

Thank You for providing for me. Today, I am thankful for...

_____
_____
_____
_____

> And forgive us our debts, as we forgive our debtors.

I need Your forgiveness...
Who do I need to forgive today, Father?...

_____
_____
_____
_____

> And lead us not into temptation,
> but deliver us from evil:
> For thine is the kingdom,
> and the power, and the glory, for ever.

I need Your protection and rescue...

_____
_____
_____
_____

Thank You, Father, for hearing my prayers. Amen.

*The Spirit of God, who raised Jesus
from the dead, lives in you.*
ROMANS 8:11 NLT

Date:

Our Father which art in heaven, Hallowed be thy name.

God, I want my life to honor You. You have shown me Your favor in so many ways, including. . .

....
....
....
....

Thy kingdom come. Thy will be done in earth, as it is in heaven.

Please reveal Your good plans for my life. I need Your guidance in these areas. . .

....
....
....
....

Give us this day our daily bread.

Thank You for providing for me. Today, I am thankful for. . .

....
....
....
....

> And forgive us our debts,
> as we forgive our debtors.

I need Your forgiveness. . .
Who do I need to forgive today, Father? . . .

....
....
....
....

> And lead us not into temptation,
> but deliver us from evil:
> For thine is the kingdom,
> and the power, and the glory, for ever.

I need Your protection and rescue. . .

....
....
....
....

Thank You, Father, for hearing my prayers. Amen.

I call on you, my God, for you will answer me;
turn your ear to me and hear my prayer.
PSALM 17:6 NIV

Date:

Our Father which art in heaven, Hallowed be thy name.

God, I want my life to honor You. You have shown me Your favor in so many ways, including. . .

....
....
....
....

Thy kingdom come, Thy will be done in earth, as it is in heaven.

Please reveal Your good plans for my life. I need Your guidance in these areas. . .

....
....
....
....

Give us this day our daily bread.

Thank You for providing for me. Today, I am thankful for. . .

....
....
....
....

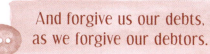

> And forgive us our debts,
> as we forgive our debtors.

I need Your forgiveness. . .
Who do I need to forgive today, Father?. . .

....
....
....
....

> And lead us not into temptation,
> but deliver us from evil:
> For thine is the kingdom,
> and the power, and the glory, for ever.

I need Your protection and rescue. . .

....
....
....
....

Thank You, Father, for hearing my prayers. Amen.

Because of the LORD's great love we are not consumed, for his compassions never fail. They are new every morning; great is your faithfulness.
LAMENTATIONS 3:22–23 NIV

Date:

Our Father which art in heaven, Hallowed be thy name.

God, I want my life to honor You. You have shown me Your favor in so many ways, including. . .

_____
_____
_____
_____

Thy kingdom come, Thy will be done in earth, as it is in heaven.

Please reveal Your good plans for my life. I need Your guidance in these areas. . .

_____
_____
_____
_____

Give us this day our daily bread.

Thank You for providing for me. Today, I am thankful for. . .

_____
_____
_____
_____

> And forgive us our debts,
> as we forgive our debtors.

I need Your forgiveness. . .
Who do I need to forgive today, Father? . . .

_____
_____
_____
_____

> And lead us not into temptation,
> but deliver us from evil:
> For thine is the kingdom,
> and the power, and the glory, for ever.

I need Your protection and rescue. . .

_____
_____
_____
_____

Thank You, Father, for hearing my prayers. Amen.

Being confident of this very thing, that he which hath begun a good work in you will perform it until the day of Jesus Christ.
PHILIPPIANS 1:6 KJV

Date:

Our Father which art in heaven, Hallowed be thy name.

God, I want my life to honor You. You have shown me Your favor in so many ways, including. . .

_____
_____
_____
_____

Thy kingdom come, Thy will be done in earth, as it is in heaven.

Please reveal Your good plans for my life. I need Your guidance in these areas. . .

_____
_____
_____
_____

Give us this day our daily bread.

Thank You for providing for me. Today, I am thankful for. . .

_____
_____
_____
_____

> And forgive us our debts,
> as we forgive our debtors.

I need Your forgiveness...
Who do I need to forgive today, Father?...

....
....
....
....

> And lead us not into temptation,
> but deliver us from evil:
> For thine is the kingdom,
> and the power, and the glory, for ever.

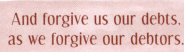

I need Your protection and rescue...

....
....
....
....

Thank You, Father, for hearing my prayers. Amen.

*Pray that I may declare [the gospel]
fearlessly, as I should.*
EPHESIANS 6:20 NIV

Date:

Our Father which art in heaven, Hallowed be thy name.

God, I want my life to honor You. You have shown me Your favor in so many ways, including...

....
....
....

Thy kingdom come, Thy will be done in earth, as it is in heaven.

Please reveal Your good plans for my life. I need Your guidance in these areas...

....
....
....
....

Give us this day our daily bread.

Thank You for providing for me. Today, I am thankful for...

....
....
....
....

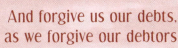

> And forgive us our debts,
> as we forgive our debtors.

I need Your forgiveness. . .
Who do I need to forgive today, Father?. . .

_____
_____
_____
_____

> And lead us not into temptation,
> but deliver us from evil:
> For thine is the kingdom,
> and the power, and the glory, for ever.

I need Your protection and rescue. . .

_____
_____
_____
_____

Thank You, Father, for hearing my prayers. Amen.

As the deer pants for streams of water, so my soul pants for you, my God. My soul thirsts for God, for the living God. When can I go and meet with God?
PSALM 42:1–2 NIV

Date:

Our Father which art in heaven, Hallowed be thy name.

God, I want my life to honor You. You have shown me Your favor in so many ways, including. . .

....
....
....
....

Thy kingdom come, Thy will be done in earth, as it is in heaven.

Please reveal Your good plans for my life. I need Your guidance in these areas. . .

....
....
....
....

Give us this day our daily bread.

Thank You for providing for me. Today, I am thankful for. . .

....
....
....
....

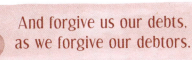

> And forgive us our debts,
> as we forgive our debtors.

I need Your forgiveness. . .
Who do I need to forgive today, Father?. . .

_____
_____
_____
_____

> And lead us not into temptation,
> but deliver us from evil:
> For thine is the kingdom,
> and the power, and the glory, for ever.

I need Your protection and rescue. . .

_____
_____
_____
_____

Thank You, Father, for hearing my prayers. Amen.

*Why, my soul, are you downcast? Why so
disturbed within me? Put your hope in God, for
I will yet praise him, my Savior and my God.*
PSALM 42:11 NIV

Date:

Our Father which art in heaven, Hallowed be thy name.

God, I want my life to honor You. You have shown me Your favor in so many ways, including. . .

....
....
....
....

Thy kingdom come, Thy will be done in earth, as it is in heaven.

Please reveal Your good plans for my life. I need Your guidance in these areas. . .

....
....
....
....

Give us this day our daily bread.

Thank You for providing for me. Today, I am thankful for. . .

....
....
....
....

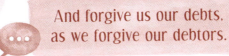

And forgive us our debts, as we forgive our debtors.

I need Your forgiveness...
Who do I need to forgive today, Father?...

_____
_____
_____
_____

And lead us not into temptation, but deliver us from evil: For thine is the kingdom, and the power, and the glory, for ever.

I need Your protection and rescue...

_____
_____
_____
_____

Thank You, Father, for hearing my prayers. Amen.

> "O LORD, God of Israel, there is no God like you in all of heaven and earth. You keep your covenant and show unfailing love to all who walk before you in wholehearted devotion."
> 2 CHRONICLES 6:14 NLT

Date:

Our Father which art in heaven, Hallowed be thy name.

God, I want my life to honor You. You have shown me Your favor in so many ways, including. . .

....
....
....
....

Thy kingdom come. Thy will be done in earth, as it is in heaven.

Please reveal Your good plans for my life. I need Your guidance in these areas. . .

....
....
....
....

Give us this day our daily bread.

Thank You for providing for me. Today, I am thankful for. . .

....
....
....
....

> And forgive us our debts,
> as we forgive our debtors.

I need Your forgiveness...
Who do I need to forgive today, Father?...

_____
_____
_____
_____

> And lead us not into temptation,
> but deliver us from evil:
> For thine is the kingdom,
> and the power, and the glory, for ever.

I need Your protection and rescue...

_____
_____
_____
_____

Thank You, Father, for hearing my prayers. Amen.

"The God we serve is able to deliver us."
DANIEL 3:17 NIV

Date:

Our Father which art in heaven, Hallowed be thy name.

God, I want my life to honor You. You have shown me Your favor in so many ways, including. . .

....
....
....
....

Thy kingdom come. Thy will be done in earth, as it is in heaven.

Please reveal Your good plans for my life. I need Your guidance in these areas. . .

....
....
....
....

Give us this day our daily bread.

Thank You for providing for me. Today, I am thankful for. . .

....
....
....
....

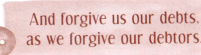

> And forgive us our debts, as we forgive our debtors.

I need Your forgiveness...
Who do I need to forgive today, Father?...

> And lead us not into temptation,
> but deliver us from evil:
> For thine is the kingdom,
> and the power, and the glory, for ever.

I need Your protection and rescue...

Thank You, Father, for hearing my prayers. Amen.

"I have told you these things, so that in me you may have peace. In this world you will have trouble. But take heart! I have overcome the world."
JOHN 16:33 NIV

Date:

Our Father which art in heaven, Hallowed be thy name.

God, I want my life to honor You. You have shown me Your favor in so many ways, including. . .

....
....
....
....

Thy kingdom come. Thy will be done in earth, as it is in heaven.

Please reveal Your good plans for my life. I need Your guidance in these areas. . .

....
....
....
....

Give us this day our daily bread.

Thank You for providing for me. Today, I am thankful for. . .

....
....
....
....

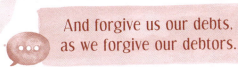

> And forgive us our debts,
> as we forgive our debtors.

I need Your forgiveness. . .
Who do I need to forgive today, Father? . . .

_____
_____
_____
_____

> And lead us not into temptation,
> but deliver us from evil:
> For thine is the kingdom,
> and the power, and the glory, for ever.

I need Your protection and rescue. . .

_____
_____
_____
_____

Thank You, Father, for hearing my prayers. Amen.

*And we know that in all things God works
for the good of those who love him, who have
been called according to his purpose.*
ROMANS 8:28 NIV

Date:

Our Father which art in heaven, Hallowed be thy name.

God, I want my life to honor You. You have shown me Your favor in so many ways, including. . .

....
....
....
....

Thy kingdom come, Thy will be done in earth, as it is in heaven.

Please reveal Your good plans for my life. I need Your guidance in these areas. . .

....
....
....
....

Give us this day our daily bread.

Thank You for providing for me. Today, I am thankful for. . .

....
....
....
....

> And forgive us our debts,
> as we forgive our debtors.

I need Your forgiveness. . .
Who do I need to forgive today, Father?. . .

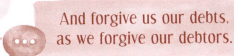

> And lead us not into temptation,
> but deliver us from evil:
> For thine is the kingdom,
> and the power, and the glory, for ever.

I need Your protection and rescue. . .

Thank You, Father, for hearing my prayers. Amen.

*For the LORD gives wisdom; from his mouth
come knowledge and understanding.*
PROVERBS 2:6 NIV

Date:

Our Father which art in heaven, Hallowed be thy name.

God, I want my life to honor You. You have shown me Your favor in so many ways, including...

....
....
....
....

Thy kingdom come, Thy will be done in earth, as it is in heaven.

Please reveal Your good plans for my life. I need Your guidance in these areas...

....
....
....
....

Give us this day our daily bread.

Thank You for providing for me. Today, I am thankful for...

....
....
....
....

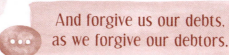

> And forgive us our debts,
> as we forgive our debtors.

I need Your forgiveness. . .
Who do I need to forgive today, Father? . . .

....

....

....

....

> And lead us not into temptation,
> but deliver us from evil:
> For thine is the kingdom,
> and the power, and the glory, for ever.

I need Your protection and rescue. . .

....

....

....

....

Thank You, Father, for hearing my prayers. Amen.

*Blessed is the one. . .whose delight is in the law of the
LORD, and who meditates on his law day and night.*
PSALM 1:1–2 NIV

Date: _____

Our Father which art in heaven, Hallowed be thy name.

God, I want my life to honor You. You have shown me Your favor in so many ways, including. . .

_____
_____
_____
_____

Thy kingdom come, Thy will be done in earth, as it is in heaven.

Please reveal Your good plans for my life. I need Your guidance in these areas. . .

_____
_____
_____
_____

Give us this day our daily bread.

Thank You for providing for me. Today, I am thankful for. . .

_____
_____
_____
_____

> And forgive us our debts,
> as we forgive our debtors.

I need Your forgiveness. . .
Who do I need to forgive today, Father? . . .

_____
_____
_____
_____

> And lead us not into temptation,
> but deliver us from evil:
> For thine is the kingdom,
> and the power, and the glory, for ever.

I need Your protection and rescue. . .

_____
_____
_____
_____

Thank You, Father, for hearing my prayers. Amen.

Finally, be strong in the Lord and in his mighty power.
EPHESIANS 6:10 NIV

Date:

Our Father which art in heaven, Hallowed be thy name.

God, I want my life to honor You. You have shown me Your favor in so many ways, including. . .

....
....
....
....

Thy kingdom come, Thy will be done in earth, as it is in heaven.

Please reveal Your good plans for my life. I need Your guidance in these areas. . .

....
....
....
....

Give us this day our daily bread.

Thank You for providing for me. Today, I am thankful for. . .

....
....
....
....

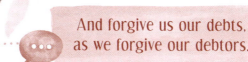

> And forgive us our debts,
> as we forgive our debtors.

I need Your forgiveness...
Who do I need to forgive today, Father?...

> And lead us not into temptation,
> but deliver us from evil:
> For thine is the kingdom,
> and the power, and the glory, for ever.

I need Your protection and rescue...

Thank You, Father, for hearing my prayers. Amen.

LORD, save us! LORD, grant us success!
Blessed is he who comes in the name of the LORD.
From the house of the LORD we bless you.
PSALM 118:25–26 NIV

Date:

Our Father which art in heaven, Hallowed be thy name.

God, I want my life to honor You. You have shown me Your favor in so many ways, including. . .

....
....
....

Thy kingdom come. Thy will be done in earth, as it is in heaven.

Please reveal Your good plans for my life. I need Your guidance in these areas. . .

....
....
....
....

Give us this day our daily bread.

Thank You for providing for me. Today, I am thankful for. . .

....
....
....
....

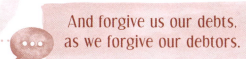

> And forgive us our debts,
> as we forgive our debtors.

I need Your forgiveness. . .
Who do I need to forgive today, Father? . . .

_____
_____
_____
_____

> And lead us not into temptation,
> but deliver us from evil:
> For thine is the kingdom,
> and the power, and the glory, for ever.

I need Your protection and rescue. . .

_____
_____
_____
_____

Thank You, Father, for hearing my prayers. Amen.

May these words of my mouth and this
meditation of my heart be pleasing in your
sight, LORD, my Rock and my Redeemer.
PSALM 19:14 NIV

Date:

Our Father which art in heaven, Hallowed be thy name.

God, I want my life to honor You. You have shown me Your favor in so many ways, including. . .

....
....
....
....

Thy kingdom come, Thy will be done in earth, as it is in heaven.

Please reveal Your good plans for my life. I need Your guidance in these areas. . .

....
....
....
....

Give us this day our daily bread.

Thank You for providing for me. Today, I am thankful for. . .

....
....
....
....

> **And forgive us our debts, as we forgive our debtors.**

I need Your forgiveness. . .
Who do I need to forgive today, Father? . . .

....
....
....
....

> **And lead us not into temptation, but deliver us from evil: For thine is the kingdom, and the power, and the glory, for ever.**

I need Your protection and rescue. . .

....
....
....
....

Thank You, Father, for hearing my prayers. Amen.

I pray to you, O LORD. I say, "You are my place of refuge. You are all I really want in life."
PSALM 142:5 NLT

Date:

Our Father which art in heaven, Hallowed be thy name.

God, I want my life to honor You. You have shown me Your favor in so many ways, including. . .

....
....
....
....

Thy kingdom come. Thy will be done in earth, as it is in heaven.

Please reveal Your good plans for my life. I need Your guidance in these areas. . .

....
....
....
....

Give us this day our daily bread.

Thank You for providing for me. Today, I am thankful for. . .

....
....
....
....

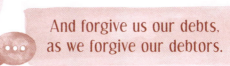

> And forgive us our debts,
> as we forgive our debtors.

I need Your forgiveness...
Who do I need to forgive today, Father?...

....

....

....

> And lead us not into temptation,
> but deliver us from evil:
> For thine is the kingdom,
> and the power, and the glory, for ever.

I need Your protection and rescue...

....

....

....

....

Thank You, Father, for hearing my prayers. Amen.

For you make me glad by your deeds, LORD; I sing for joy at what your hands have done. How great are your works, LORD, how profound your thoughts!
PSALM 92:4–5 NIV

Date:

Our Father which art in heaven, Hallowed be thy name.

God, I want my life to honor You. You have shown me Your favor in so many ways, including. . .

....
....
....
....

Thy kingdom come, Thy will be done in earth, as it is in heaven.

Please reveal Your good plans for my life. I need Your guidance in these areas. . .

....
....
....
....

Give us this day our daily bread.

Thank You for providing for me. Today, I am thankful for. . .

....
....
....
....

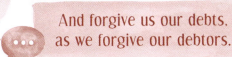

> And forgive us our debts,
> as we forgive our debtors.

I need Your forgiveness. . .
Who do I need to forgive today, Father? . . .

_____
_____
_____
_____

> And lead us not into temptation,
> but deliver us from evil:
> For thine is the kingdom,
> and the power, and the glory, for ever.

I need Your protection and rescue. . .

_____
_____
_____
_____

Thank You, Father, for hearing my prayers. Amen.

*My intercessor is my friend as my
eyes pour out tears to God.*
JOB 16:20 NIV

Date:

Our Father which art in heaven, Hallowed be thy name.

God, I want my life to honor You. You have shown me Your favor in so many ways, including. . .

....
....
....
....

Thy kingdom come, Thy will be done in earth, as it is in heaven.

Please reveal Your good plans for my life. I need Your guidance in these areas. . .

....
....
....
....

Give us this day our daily bread.

Thank You for providing for me. Today, I am thankful for. . .

....
....
....
....

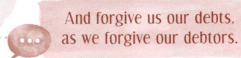

And forgive us our debts,
as we forgive our debtors.

I need Your forgiveness. . .
Who do I need to forgive today, Father? . . .

_____

_____

_____

_____

And lead us not into temptation,
but deliver us from evil:
For thine is the kingdom,
and the power, and the glory, for ever.

I need Your protection and rescue. . .

_____

_____

_____

_____

Thank You, Father, for hearing my prayers. Amen.

Rejoice in the Lord always. I will say it again: Rejoice!
PHILIPPIANS 4:4 NIV

Date:

Our Father which art in heaven, Hallowed be thy name.

God, I want my life to honor You. You have shown me Your favor in so many ways, including...

_____
_____
_____
_____

Thy kingdom come. Thy will be done in earth, as it is in heaven.

Please reveal Your good plans for my life. I need Your guidance in these areas...

_____
_____
_____
_____

Give us this day our daily bread.

Thank You for providing for me. Today, I am thankful for...

_____
_____
_____
_____

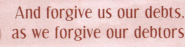

And forgive us our debts, as we forgive our debtors.

I need Your forgiveness...
Who do I need to forgive today, Father?...

_____

_____

_____

_____

And lead us not into temptation, but deliver us from evil: For thine is the kingdom, and the power, and the glory, for ever.

I need Your protection and rescue...

_____

_____

_____

_____

Thank You, Father, for hearing my prayers. Amen.

> "Ask and it will be given to you; seek and you will find; knock and the door will be opened to you. For everyone who asks receives; the one who seeks finds; and to the one who knocks, the door will be opened."
> MATTHEW 7:7–8 NIV

Date:

Our Father which art in heaven, Hallowed be thy name.

God, I want my life to honor You. You have shown me Your favor in so many ways, including. . .

....
....
....
....

Thy kingdom come. Thy will be done in earth, as it is in heaven.

Please reveal Your good plans for my life. I need Your guidance in these areas. . .

....
....
....
....

Give us this day our daily bread.

Thank You for providing for me. Today, I am thankful for. . .

....
....
....
....

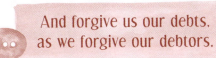

> And forgive us our debts, as we forgive our debtors.

I need Your forgiveness...
Who do I need to forgive today, Father?...

> And lead us not into temptation, but deliver us from evil:
> For thine is the kingdom, and the power, and the glory, for ever.

I need Your protection and rescue...

Thank You, Father, for hearing my prayers. Amen.

> *"But blessed is the one who trusts in the LORD, whose confidence is in him."*
> JEREMIAH 17:7 NIV

Date:

Our Father which art in heaven, Hallowed be thy name.

God, I want my life to honor You. You have shown me Your favor in so many ways, including...

....
....
....
....

Thy kingdom come, Thy will be done in earth, as it is in heaven.

Please reveal Your good plans for my life. I need Your guidance in these areas...

....
....
....
....

Give us this day our daily bread.

Thank You for providing for me. Today, I am thankful for...

....
....
....
....

> And forgive us our debts, as we forgive our debtors.

I need Your forgiveness. . .
Who do I need to forgive today, Father? . . .

....
....
....
....

> And lead us not into temptation, but deliver us from evil:
> For thine is the kingdom, and the power, and the glory, for ever.

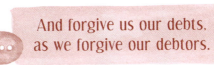

I need Your protection and rescue. . .

....
....
....
....

Thank You, Father, for hearing my prayers. Amen.

"The LORD is my portion; therefore I will wait for him."
LAMENTATIONS 3:24 NIV

Date:

Our Father which art in heaven, Hallowed be thy name.

God, I want my life to honor You. You have shown me Your favor in so many ways, including. . .

_____
_____
_____
_____

Thy kingdom come. Thy will be done in earth, as it is in heaven.

Please reveal Your good plans for my life. I need Your guidance in these areas. . .

_____
_____
_____
_____

Give us this day our daily bread.

Thank You for providing for me. Today, I am thankful for. . .

_____
_____
_____
_____

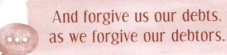

> And forgive us our debts,
> as we forgive our debtors.

I need Your forgiveness...
Who do I need to forgive today, Father?...

_____

_____

_____

_____

> And lead us not into temptation,
> but deliver us from evil:
> For thine is the kingdom,
> and the power, and the glory, for ever.

I need Your protection and rescue...

_____

_____

_____

_____

Thank You, Father, for hearing my prayers. Amen.

> "As the heavens are higher than the earth,
> so are my ways higher than your ways and
> my thoughts than your thoughts."
> ISAIAH 55:9 NIV

Date:

Our Father which art in heaven, Hallowed be thy name.

God, I want my life to honor You. You have shown me Your favor in so many ways, including. . .

....
....
....
....

Thy kingdom come, Thy will be done in earth, as it is in heaven.

Please reveal Your good plans for my life. I need Your guidance in these areas. . .

....
....
....
....

Give us this day our daily bread.

Thank You for providing for me. Today, I am thankful for. . .

....
....
....
....

> **And forgive us our debts,
> as we forgive our debtors.**

I need Your forgiveness. . .
Who do I need to forgive today, Father? . . .

_____
_____
_____
_____

> **And lead us not into temptation,
> but deliver us from evil:
> For thine is the kingdom,
> and the power, and the glory, for ever.**

I need Your protection and rescue. . .

_____
_____
_____
_____

Thank You, Father, for hearing my prayers. Amen.

*But I'm in the very presence of God—
oh, how refreshing it is!*
PSALM 73:27 MSG

Date:

Our Father which art in heaven. Hallowed be thy name.

God, I want my life to honor You. You have shown me Your favor in so many ways, including. . .

....
....
....
....

Thy kingdom come. Thy will be done in earth, as it is in heaven.

Please reveal Your good plans for my life. I need Your guidance in these areas. . .

....
....
....
....

Give us this day our daily bread.

Thank You for providing for me. Today, I am thankful for. . .

....
....
....
....

> And forgive us our debts,
> as we forgive our debtors.

I need Your forgiveness...
Who do I need to forgive today, Father?...

> And lead us not into temptation,
> but deliver us from evil:
> For thine is the kingdom,
> and the power, and the glory, for ever.

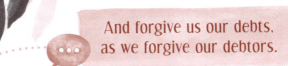

I need Your protection and rescue...

Thank You, Father, for hearing my prayers. Amen.

*Devote yourselves to prayer with an
alert mind and a thankful heart.*
COLOSSIANS 4:2 NLT

Date:

Our Father which art in heaven, Hallowed be thy name.

God, I want my life to honor You. You have shown me Your favor in so many ways, including...

....
....
....
....

Thy kingdom come. Thy will be done in earth, as it is in heaven.

Please reveal Your good plans for my life. I need Your guidance in these areas...

....
....
....
....

Give us this day our daily bread.

Thank You for providing for me. Today, I am thankful for...

....
....
....
....

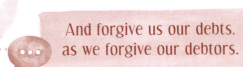

> And forgive us our debts,
> as we forgive our debtors.

I need Your forgiveness. . .
Who do I need to forgive today, Father? . . .

....
....
....
....

> And lead us not into temptation,
> but deliver us from evil:
> For thine is the kingdom,
> and the power, and the glory, for ever.

I need Your protection and rescue. . .

....
....
....
....

Thank You, Father, for hearing my prayers. Amen.

But each day the LORD pours his unfailing love upon me, and through each night I sing his songs, praying to God who gives me life.
PSALM 42:8 NLT

Date:

Our Father which art in heaven, Hallowed be thy name.

God, I want my life to honor You. You have shown me Your favor in so many ways, including. . .

....
....
....
....

Thy kingdom come, Thy will be done in earth, as it is in heaven.

Please reveal Your good plans for my life. I need Your guidance in these areas. . .

....
....
....
....

Give us this day our daily bread.

Thank You for providing for me. Today, I am thankful for. . .

....
....
....
....

> And forgive us our debts,
> as we forgive our debtors.

I need Your forgiveness. . .
Who do I need to forgive today, Father? . . .

> And lead us not into temptation,
> but deliver us from evil:
> For thine is the kingdom,
> and the power, and the glory, for ever.

I need Your protection and rescue. . .

Thank You, Father, for hearing my prayers. Amen.

"Pray with all your might! And don't let up!"
1 SAMUEL 7:8 MSG

Date:

Our Father which art in heaven, Hallowed be thy name.

God, I want my life to honor You. You have shown me Your favor in so many ways, including. . .

....
....
....
....

Thy kingdom come, Thy will be done in earth, as it is in heaven.

Please reveal Your good plans for my life. I need Your guidance in these areas. . .

....
....
....
....

Give us this day our daily bread.

Thank You for providing for me. Today, I am thankful for. . .

....
....
....
....

> And forgive us our debts,
> as we forgive our debtors.

I need Your forgiveness...
Who do I need to forgive today, Father?...

_____
_____
_____
_____

> And lead us not into temptation,
> but deliver us from evil:
> For thine is the kingdom,
> and the power, and the glory, for ever.

I need Your protection and rescue...

_____
_____
_____
_____

Thank You, Father, for hearing my prayers. Amen.

*Answer my prayers, O Lord,
for your unfailing love is wonderful.*
PSALM 69:16 NLT

Date:

Our Father which art in heaven, Hallowed be thy name.

God, I want my life to honor You. You have shown me Your favor in so many ways, including. . .

....
....
....
....

Thy kingdom come, Thy will be done in earth, as it is in heaven.

Please reveal Your good plans for my life. I need Your guidance in these areas. . .

....
....
....
....

Give us this day our daily bread.

Thank You for providing for me. Today, I am thankful for. . .

....
....
....
....

> And forgive us our debts, as we forgive our debtors.

I need Your forgiveness...
Who do I need to forgive today, Father?...

_____
_____
_____
_____

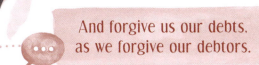

> And lead us not into temptation, but deliver us from evil: For thine is the kingdom, and the power, and the glory, for ever.

I need Your protection and rescue...

_____
_____
_____
_____

Thank You, Father, for hearing my prayers. Amen.

They will pray for you with deep affection because of the overflowing grace God has given to you.
2 CORINTHIANS 9:14 NLT

Date:

Our Father which art in heaven, Hallowed be thy name.

God, I want my life to honor You. You have shown me Your favor in so many ways, including. . .

....
....
....
....

Thy kingdom come, Thy will be done in earth, as it is in heaven.

Please reveal Your good plans for my life. I need Your guidance in these areas. . .

....
....
....
....

Give us this day our daily bread.

Thank You for providing for me. Today, I am thankful for. . .

....
....
....
....

> And forgive us our debts,
> as we forgive our debtors.

I need Your forgiveness...
Who do I need to forgive today, Father?...

> And lead us not into temptation,
> but deliver us from evil:
> For thine is the kingdom,
> and the power, and the glory, for ever.

I need Your protection and rescue...

Thank You, Father, for hearing my prayers. Amen.

*Because he bends down to listen,
I will pray as long as I have breath!*
PSALM 116:2 NLT

Date:

Our Father which art in heaven, Hallowed be thy name.

God, I want my life to honor You. You have shown me Your favor in so many ways, including. . .

_____
_____
_____
_____

Thy kingdom come, Thy will be done in earth, as it is in heaven.

Please reveal Your good plans for my life. I need Your guidance in these areas. . .

_____
_____
_____
_____

Give us this day our daily bread.

Thank You for providing for me. Today, I am thankful for. . .

_____
_____
_____
_____

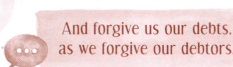

> And forgive us our debts,
> as we forgive our debtors.

I need Your forgiveness...
Who do I need to forgive today, Father?...

> And lead us not into temptation,
> but deliver us from evil:
> For thine is the kingdom,
> and the power, and the glory, for ever.

I need Your protection and rescue...

Thank You, Father, for hearing my prayers. Amen.

Hallelujah! O my soul, praise GOD! All my life long I'll praise GOD, singing songs to my God as long as I live.
PSALM 146:1–2 MSG

Date: _____

Our Father which art in heaven, Hallowed be thy name.

God, I want my life to honor You. You have shown me Your favor in so many ways, including. . .

....
....
....
....

Thy kingdom come, Thy will be done in earth, as it is in heaven.

Please reveal Your good plans for my life. I need Your guidance in these areas. . .

....
....
....
....

Give us this day our daily bread.

Thank You for providing for me. Today, I am thankful for. . .

....
....
....
....

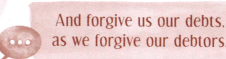

> And forgive us our debts,
> as we forgive our debtors.

I need Your forgiveness...
Who do I need to forgive today, Father?...

> And lead us not into temptation,
> but deliver us from evil:
> For thine is the kingdom,
> and the power, and the glory, for ever.

I need Your protection and rescue...

Thank You, Father, for hearing my prayers. Amen.

I pray that from his glorious, unlimited resources he will empower you with inner strength through his Spirit.
EPHESIANS 3:16 NLT

Date:

Our Father which art in heaven, Hallowed be thy name.

God, I want my life to honor You. You have shown me Your favor in so many ways, including...

Thy kingdom come. Thy will be done in earth, as it is in heaven.

Please reveal Your good plans for my life. I need Your guidance in these areas...

Give us this day our daily bread.

Thank You for providing for me. Today, I am thankful for...

> And forgive us our debts,
> as we forgive our debtors.

I need Your forgiveness. . .
Who do I need to forgive today, Father? . . .

> And lead us not into temptation,
> but deliver us from evil:
> For thine is the kingdom,
> and the power, and the glory, for ever.

I need Your protection and rescue. . .

Thank You, Father, for hearing my prayers. Amen.

*I lift my hands to you in prayer. I thirst for
you as parched land thirsts for rain.*
PSALM 143:6 NLT

Date:

Our Father which art in heaven, Hallowed be thy name.

God, I want my life to honor You. You have shown me Your favor in so many ways, including. . .

....
....
....

Thy kingdom come. Thy will be done in earth, as it is in heaven.

Please reveal Your good plans for my life. I need Your guidance in these areas. . .

....
....
....
....

Give us this day our daily bread.

Thank You for providing for me. Today, I am thankful for. . .

....
....
....
....

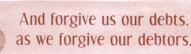

And forgive us our debts, as we forgive our debtors.

I need Your forgiveness. . .
Who do I need to forgive today, Father? . . .

....
....
....
....

And lead us not into temptation, but deliver us from evil: For thine is the kingdom, and the power, and the glory, for ever.

I need Your protection and rescue. . .

....
....
....
....

Thank You, Father, for hearing my prayers. Amen.

Bless those who curse you. Pray for those who hurt you.
LUKE 6:28 NLT

Date:

Our Father which art in heaven, Hallowed be thy name.

God, I want my life to honor You. You have shown me Your favor in so many ways, including. . .

....
....
....
....

Thy kingdom come, Thy will be done in earth, as it is in heaven.

Please reveal Your good plans for my life. I need Your guidance in these areas. . .

....
....
....
....

Give us this day our daily bread.

Thank You for providing for me. Today, I am thankful for. . .

....
....
....
....

And forgive us our debts, as we forgive our debtors.

I need Your forgiveness. . .
Who do I need to forgive today, Father? . . .

And lead us not into temptation, but deliver us from evil: For thine is the kingdom, and the power, and the glory, for ever.

I need Your protection and rescue. . .

Thank You, Father, for hearing my prayers. Amen.

I pray that your love will overflow more and more, and that you will keep on growing in knowledge and understanding.
PHILIPPIANS 1:9 NLT

Date:

Our Father which art in heaven, Hallowed be thy name.

God, I want my life to honor You. You have shown me Your favor in so many ways, including...

....
....
....

Thy kingdom come. Thy will be done in earth, as it is in heaven.

Please reveal Your good plans for my life. I need Your guidance in these areas...

....
....
....

Give us this day our daily bread.

Thank You for providing for me. Today, I am thankful for...

....
....
....

> And forgive us our debts, as we forgive our debtors.

I need Your forgiveness...
Who do I need to forgive today, Father?...

_____

_____

_____

_____

> And lead us not into temptation,
> but deliver us from evil:
> For thine is the kingdom,
> and the power, and the glory, for ever.

I need Your protection and rescue...

_____

_____

_____

_____

Thank You, Father, for hearing my prayers. Amen.

I pray to you, O LORD, my rock.
PSALM 28:1 NLT

Date:

Our Father which art in heaven, Hallowed be thy name.

God, I want my life to honor You. You have shown me Your favor in so many ways, including...

....
....
....
....

Thy kingdom come. Thy will be done in earth, as it is in heaven.

Please reveal Your good plans for my life. I need Your guidance in these areas...

....
....
....
....

Give us this day our daily bread.

Thank You for providing for me. Today, I am thankful for...

....
....
....
....

> And forgive us our debts,
> as we forgive our debtors.

I need Your forgiveness...
Who do I need to forgive today, Father?...

....
....
....
....

> And lead us not into temptation,
> but deliver us from evil:
> For thine is the kingdom,
> and the power, and the glory, for ever.

I need Your protection and rescue...

....
....
....
....

Thank You, Father, for hearing my prayers. Amen.

*You're my place of quiet retreat;
I wait for your Word to renew me.*
PSALM 119:113 MSG

Date:

Our Father which art in heaven, Hallowed be thy name.

God, I want my life to honor You. You have shown me Your favor in so many ways, including. . .

....
....
....
....

Thy kingdom come. Thy will be done in earth, as it is in heaven.

Please reveal Your good plans for my life. I need Your guidance in these areas. . .

....
....
....
....

Give us this day our daily bread.

Thank You for providing for me. Today, I am thankful for. . .

....
....
....
....

> And forgive us our debts,
> as we forgive our debtors.

I need Your forgiveness...
Who do I need to forgive today, Father?...

_____
_____
_____
_____

> And lead us not into temptation,
> but deliver us from evil:
> For thine is the kingdom,
> and the power, and the glory, for ever.

I need Your protection and rescue...

_____
_____
_____
_____

Thank You, Father, for hearing my prayers. Amen.

In your unfailing love, O God, answer my prayer with your sure salvation.
PSALM 69:13 NLT

Date:

Our Father which art in heaven, Hallowed be thy name.

God, I want my life to honor You. You have shown me Your favor in so many ways, including...

....
....
....
....

Thy kingdom come, Thy will be done in earth, as it is in heaven.

Please reveal Your good plans for my life. I need Your guidance in these areas...

....
....
....
....

Give us this day our daily bread.

Thank You for providing for me. Today, I am thankful for...

....
....
....
....

And forgive us our debts, as we forgive our debtors.

I need Your forgiveness. . .
Who do I need to forgive today, Father? . . .

And lead us not into temptation, but deliver us from evil: For thine is the kingdom, and the power, and the glory, for ever.

I need Your protection and rescue. . .

Thank You, Father, for hearing my prayers. Amen.

Be joyful in hope, patient in affliction, faithful in prayer.
ROMANS 12:12 NIV

Date:

Our Father which art in heaven, Hallowed be thy name.

God, I want my life to honor You. You have shown me Your favor in so many ways, including. . .

....
....
....
....

Thy kingdom come, Thy will be done in earth, as it is in heaven.

Please reveal Your good plans for my life. I need Your guidance in these areas. . .

....
....
....
....

Give us this day our daily bread.

Thank You for providing for me. Today, I am thankful for. . .

....
....
....
....

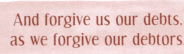

> And forgive us our debts,
> as we forgive our debtors.

I need Your forgiveness. . .
Who do I need to forgive today, Father?. . .

_____
_____
_____
_____

> And lead us not into temptation,
> but deliver us from evil:
> For thine is the kingdom,
> and the power, and the glory, for ever.

I need Your protection and rescue. . .

_____
_____
_____
_____

Thank You, Father, for hearing my prayers. Amen.

God, the one and only. . .Everything I hope for comes from him. . . . He's solid rock under my feet, breathing room for my soul. . .I'm set for life.
PSALM 62:5–6 MSG

Date:

Our Father which art in heaven, Hallowed be thy name.

God, I want my life to honor You. You have shown me Your favor in so many ways, including. . .

_____
_____
_____
_____

Thy kingdom come, Thy will be done in earth, as it is in heaven.

Please reveal Your good plans for my life. I need Your guidance in these areas. . .

_____
_____
_____
_____

Give us this day our daily bread.

Thank You for providing for me. Today, I am thankful for. . .

_____
_____
_____
_____

> And forgive us our debts,
> as we forgive our debtors.

I need Your forgiveness. . .
Who do I need to forgive today, Father? . . .

_____
_____
_____
_____

> And lead us not into temptation,
> but deliver us from evil:
> For thine is the kingdom,
> and the power, and the glory, for ever.

I need Your protection and rescue. . .

_____
_____
_____
_____

Thank You, Father, for hearing my prayers. Amen.

Let your unfailing love surround us,
LORD, for our hope is in you alone.
PSALM 33:22 NLT

Date:

Our Father which art in heaven, Hallowed be thy name.

God, I want my life to honor You. You have shown me Your favor in so many ways, including. . .

....
....
....

Thy kingdom come, Thy will be done in earth, as it is in heaven.

Please reveal Your good plans for my life. I need Your guidance in these areas. . .

....
....
....

Give us this day our daily bread.

Thank You for providing for me. Today, I am thankful for. . .

....
....
....
....

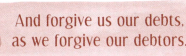

And forgive us our debts, as we forgive our debtors.

I need Your forgiveness. . .
Who do I need to forgive today, Father? . . .

And lead us not into temptation, but deliver us from evil: For thine is the kingdom, and the power, and the glory, for ever.

I need Your protection and rescue. . .

Thank You, Father, for hearing my prayers. Amen.

Guide me in your truth and teach me, for you are God my Savior, and my hope is in you all day long.
PSALM 25:5 NIV

Date:

Our Father which art in heaven, Hallowed be thy name.

God, I want my life to honor You. You have shown me Your favor in so many ways, including...

....
....
....
....

Thy kingdom come, Thy will be done in earth, as it is in heaven.

Please reveal Your good plans for my life. I need Your guidance in these areas...

....
....
....
....

Give us this day our daily bread.

Thank You for providing for me. Today, I am thankful for...

....
....
....
....

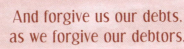

And forgive us our debts,
as we forgive our debtors.

I need Your forgiveness. . .
Who do I need to forgive today, Father?. . .

_____

_____

_____

_____

And lead us not into temptation,
but deliver us from evil:
For thine is the kingdom,
and the power, and the glory, for ever.

I need Your protection and rescue. . .

_____

_____

_____

_____

Thank You, Father, for hearing my prayers. Amen.

Now ask and keep on asking and you will receive, so that your joy (gladness, delight) may be full and complete.
JOHN 16:24 AMPC

Discover More Faith Maps for the Entire Family...

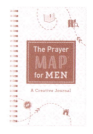

The Prayer Map for Men
978-1-64352-438-2

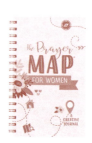

The Prayer Map for Women
978-1-68322-557-7

The Prayer Map for Girls
978-1-68322-559-1

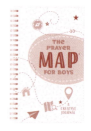

The Prayer Map for Boys
978-1-68322-558-4

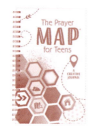

The Prayer Map for Teens
978-1-68322-556-0

These purposeful prayer journals are a fun and creative way to more fully experience the power of prayer. Each page guides you to write out thoughts, ideas, and lists...which then creates a specific "map" for you to follow as you talk to God. Each map includes a spot to record the date, so you can look back on your prayers and see how God has worked in your life. *The Prayer Map* will not only encourage you to spend time talking with God about the things that matter most...it will also help you build a healthy spiritual habit of continual prayer for life!

Find This and More from Barbour Publishing at Your Favorite Bookstore or www.barbourbooks.com